# BABY'S *first* Tattoo

## A Memory Book
## for Modern Parents

# JIM MULLEN

## Illustrations by Barry Blitt

BLOOMSBURY

First published in Great Britain 2004

Text copyright © 2002 by Jim Mullen

Illustrations copyright © 2002 by Barry Blitt

The moral right of the authors has been asserted

Designed by Bonni Leon Berman/Katie Tooke

Bloomsbury Publishing, Plc, 38 Soho Square, London W1D 3HB

A CIP catalogue record for this book is available from the British Library

ISBN 0-7475-6920-7

1 3 5 7 9 10 8 6 4 2

All papers used by Bloomsbury Publishing are natural, recyclable products made from
wood grown in sustainable, well-managed forests. The manufacturing processes conform
to the environmental regulations of the country of origin.

Printed in China by C&C Offset Printing Co., Ltd.

# Baby's First Tattoo

 # Introduction

*T*here are two kinds of babies in the world: the cute, cuddly, cherubic bundles of joy and the real ones. This book is for parents who are thinking of having, who are near having, or who have recently had a real baby. Even if you want the other kind, chances are that you will get a real, crying, screaming, nerve-shredding baby instead.

While most books marking your baby's milestones concentrate on minor events like Baby's First Word and Baby's First Tooth, *Baby's First Tattoo* lets you relive the unforgettable moments in your baby's life that are too often ignored: Baby's First Tantrum in a Crowded Supermarket, Baby's First Dirt-Eating, Baby's First Test of Wills.

Unlike the old-fashioned baby books you will find in your parents' attic, this book is meant to be filled out beyond page four, and will also give you a timely warning as to what new hell you can expect

from your child next. Will today be the day you make two visits to A&E or just your First Panic Call to NHS Direct?

People often say to me, "If babies are such a bother and a burden, why do people keep having them?" And I say, "Because they have poor memories." To which they say, "What were we just talking about?"

The other reason is that parents, quite naturally, like to brag about their children. They play up the good things and avoid the bad. You will always hear about Billy's first step. You will rarely hear about Billy's first day in juvenile court, even if you were one of his victims. You will most definitely hear about Betty's first haircut, yet the day she bit the neighbour's kid so hard he needed stitches in his hand is somehow glossed over. *Baby's First Tattoo* presents life with a new child the way it really is, not the way it should be.

## Checklist of What to Take to the Hospital

- ☐ Video Camera
- ☐ Nightgowns
- ☐ Medicine
- ☐ Toiletry Kit
- ☐ New-Baby Books
- ☐ Slippers
- ☐ Portable CD Player (and CDs)
- ☐ Cash for TV Rental

Person Who Forgot to Take the Bag We Had Packed with All That in It . . . . . . . . . . . . . . . . . . . . . . . . . . . . . . . . . . . . . . . . . .

Baby's Home Town. . . . . . . . . . . . . . . . . . . . . . . . . . . . . . . . . . .

Hospital We Were Going to When Baby Was Born . . . . . . . . . . . . . .
. . . . . . . . . . . . . . . . . . . . . . . . . . . . . . . . . . . . . . . . . . . . . . .

Hospital Cab Driver Was Going to When Baby Was Born. . . . . . . . . .

Cause of Traffic Jam That Kept Us from Getting to the Hospital
. . . . . . . . . . . . . . . . . . . . . . . . . . . . . . . . . . . . . . . . . . . . . . .

Name of Cab Driver/Policeman Who Helped Deliver Baby. . . . . . . . . .
. . . . . . . . . . . . . . . . . . . . . . . . . . . . . . . . . . . . . . . . . . . . . . .

Nationality of Cab Driver . . . . . . . . . . . . . . . . . . . . . . . . . . . . . . . . . . . . . . . . . . . . . .

Business Trip Baby's Dad Was on While All This Happened . . . . . . . . .

. . . . . . . . . . . . . . . . . . . . . . . . . . . . . . . . . . . . . . . . . . . . . . . . . . . . . . . . . . . . . . . . . . . . . .

Why He Couldn't Have Scheduled It During the Nine Months

Before Baby Was Born . . . . . . . . . . . . . . . . . . . . . . . . . . . . . . . . . . . . . . . . . . . . .

Hours Baby's Dad Stopped Working During the Entire Pregnancy

and Delivery (if any) . . . . . . . . . . . . . . . . . . . . . . . . . . . . . . . . . . . . . . . . . . . . . . .

Chances Baby Would Be Born if Men Got Pregnant . . . . . . . . . . . . . . . .

Good Career Mum Gave Up to

Have Baby . . . . . . . . . . . . . . . . . . . . . . . .

Length of Postpartum Depression

(if over) . . . . . . . . . . . . . . . . . . . . . . . .

Name of Cab Driver Who Helped
Deliver You

# Baby's Statistics

Hair Colour . . . . . . . . . . . . . . . . . . . . . . . . . . . . . . . . . . . . . . . . . . . . . . . . . . . . .

Eye Colour . . . . . . . . . . . . . . . . . . . . . . . . . . . . . . . . . . . . . . . . . . . . . . . . . . . . . .

Weight at Birth . . . . . . . . . . . . . . . . . . . . . . . . . . . . . . . . . . . . . . . . . . . . . . . . . .

Length . . . . . . . . . . . . . . . . . . . . . . . . . . . . . . . . . . . . . . . . . . . . . . . . . . . . . . . . . .

Diameter of Baby's Head . . . . . . . . . . . . . . . . . . . . . . . . . . . . . . . . . . . . . . . . . .

Diameter of Hole Baby's Head Came Through . . . . . . . . . . . . . . . . . . . .

Saint's Name Who Administered the Epidural . . . . . . . . . . . . . . . . . . . .

Chances Mum Will Ever Do That Again . . . . . . . . . . . . . . . . . . . . . . . . . . .

Doctor Who Delivered Baby . . . . . . . . . . . . . . . . . . . . . . . . . . . . . . . . . . . . .

How Old S/he Looked . . . . . . . . . . . . . . . . . . . . . . . . . . . . . . . . . . . . . . . . . . .

Who Videotaped the Birth . . . . . . . . . . . . . . . . . . . . . . . . . . . . . . . . . . . . . . .

Who Snipped the Cord . . . . . . . . . . . . . . . . . . . . . . . . . . . . . . . . . . . . . . . . . .

Who Put the Name Tag Around Baby's Wrist . . . . . . . . . . . . . . . . . . . . .

Hours Parents Talked About This Before Mum Got Pregnant . . . . . . .

Hours Parents Talked About This After Mum Got Pregnant . . . . . . . .

What do women know about it, anyway? . . . . . . . . . . . . . . . . . . . . . . .

Did I really marry this jerk? All this palaver over a useless piece

of skin.* . . . . . . . . . . . . . . . . . . . . . . . . . . . . . . . . . . . . . . . . . . . . .

Is she kidding? A woman won't get her hair cut without a month's

thought. But you think it's OK to snip off a man's penis? . . . . . . . . . . .

. . . . . . . . . . . . . . . . . . . . . . . . . . . . . . . . . . . . . . . . . . . . . . . . . . .

Your Circumcision

* Old Joke Alert! What do you call the useless piece of skin attached to a
penis? A man.

# Baby's First Visitors

The Guy Who Fixed the Hospital TV. . . . . . . . . . . . . . . . . . . . . . . . . . . . . .

Lady Who Sold Mum Expensive "First Pictures" of New Baby . . . . . .

. . . . . . . . . . . . . . . . . . . . . . . . . . . . . . . . . . . . . . . . . . . . . . . . . . . . . . . . . . .

Flower-Delivery Guy . . . . . . . . . . . . . . . . . . . . . . . . . . . . . . . . . . . . . . . . . .

Catering Porter with Lunch . . . . . . . . . . . . . . . . . . . . . . . . . . . . . . . . . . . .

Balloon-Delivery Guy . . . . . . . . . . . . . . . . . . . . . . . . . . . . . . . . . . . . . . . . .

Baby's Doctor, if Applicable . . . . . . . . . . . . . . . . . . . . . . . . . . . . . . . . . . .

Baby's First Visitors

*The Day you came home*

Date . . . . . . . . . . . . . . . . . . . . . . . . . . . . . . . . . . . . . . . . . . . . . . . . .

Number of Days' Worth of Dishes in the Sink . . . . . . . . . . . . . . . . . . . .

Number of Empty Beer Cans Lying Around . . . . . . . . . . . . . . . . . . . . . .

Kilos of Laundry Waiting to Be Washed . . . . . . . . . . . . . . . . . . . . . . . . . .

Name of Fairy Who Dad Thinks Does All This . . . . . . . . . . . . . . . . . . . .

Number of Loads of Washing Parents Did Each Week Before Baby

Was Born . . . . . . . . . . . . . . . . . . . . . . . . . . . . . . . . . . . . . . . . . . . . . . . . .

Number of Loads of Washing Parents Do Since Baby Was Born . . . .

. . . . . . . . . . . . . . . . . . . . . . . . . . . . . . . . . . . . . . . . . . . . . . . . . . . . . . . .

## Who or What Baby Was Named After

Jewellery Store. . . . . . . . . . . . . . . . . . . . . . . . . . . . . . . . . . . . . . . . . . .

Character on *Friends* . . . . . . . . . . . . . . . . . . . . . . . . . . . . . . . . . . . .

Character on *EastEnders* . . . . . . . . . . . . . . . . . . . . . . . . . . . . . . . .

Character on *The X-Files* . . . . . . . . . . . . . . . . . . . . . . . . . . . . . . . .

New Age Guru. . . . . . . . . . . . . . . . . . . . . . . . . . . . . . . . . . . . . . . . . . .

Movie Star . . . . . . . . . . . . . . . . . . . . . . . . . . . . . . . . . . . . . . . . . . . . .

Movie Character . . . . . . . . . . . . . . . . . . . . . . . . . . . . . . . . . . . . . . . .

Pop Star. . . . . . . . . . . . . . . . . . . . . . . . . . . . . . . . . . . . . . . . . . . . . . .

Druid Priest/Priestess. . . . . . . . . . . . . . . . . . . . . . . . . . . . . . . . . . . .


Millions of Parents Who Were Thinking the Same Thing. . . . . . . . . . .

Percentage of Kids in Baby's Class Who Will Have the Same Name. .

. . . . . . . . . . . . . . . . . . . . . . . . . . . . . . . . . . . . . . . . . . . . . . . . . . . . .

How Many Times Baby Will Have to Say "That's with an 'I' Not a

'Y' " in Its Life . . . . . . . . . . . . . . . . . . . . . . . . . . . . . . . . . . . . . . . . . .

What Parents Were Drinking/Smoking When They Came Up
with It . . . . . . . . . . . . . . . . . . . . . . . . . . . . . . . . . . . . . . . . . . . . .

Relatives Who Are Still Not Talking to Parents About This . . . . . . . .

. . . . . . . . . . . . . . . . . . . . . . . . . . . . . . . . . . . . . . . . . . . . . . . . . . .

Traumatizing Nickname Baby Will Be Stuck with for Life That
Parents Never Considered Until Baby Came Home from School
Crying . . . . . . . . . . . . . . . . . . . . . . . . . . . . . . . . . . . . . . . . . . . .

"Chad"    "Prince"    "Sting"    "Deepak"    "Gladiola"

Who or what you were named after

15

# What Not to Name the Baby

## Boys

Beauregard

Cosmo

Nero

Caligula

Percy

River

Tupac

Newt

Keanu

Hannibal

Jabba

Adolf

P. Diddy

Darius

Brixton

North Dakota

Arsene

## Girls

Ethel

Guinevere

Twig

Moon Unit

Medusa

Tawnee

Fiesta

LaToya

Sky

One-Eye

Cappuccino

Maude

Ephigene

Beyoncé

Salt

Pepa

Aurora

# For Juniors Only

Junior's First Manifestation of Neurotic Behaviour . . . . . . . . . . . . . .

Junior's First Bullying Episode . . . . . . . . . . . . . . . . . . . . . . . . . . . . . .

First Time Junior Was Caught Torturing a Cat . . . . . . . . . . . . . . . . .

First Year They Held Junior Back . . . . . . . . . . . . . . . . . . . . . . . . . . . .

Junior's First Time in Juvenile Court . . . . . . . . . . . . . . . . . . . . . . . . .

Junior's Dad's Problem . . . . . . . . . . . . . . . . . . . . . . . . . . . . . . . . . . . .

Junior's Mum's Problem . . . . . . . . . . . . . . . . . . . . . . . . . . . . . . . . . . .

 # Announcements

### "Switched at Birth" Newspaper Clippings

### "Stolen from Hospital by Stranger" Newspaper Clippings

### "A-Level Dropout Posing as Midwife Delivers Baby"

Newspaper Clippings

**"Woman Gives Birth in Cab"** Newspaper Clippings

**"Surgeon Removes Wrong Leg"** at the Same Hospital You

Were in Clipping

**"Mum Survives 48-Hour Labour**

**at Local Hospital"** Baby's Birth

Announcement in Local Paper

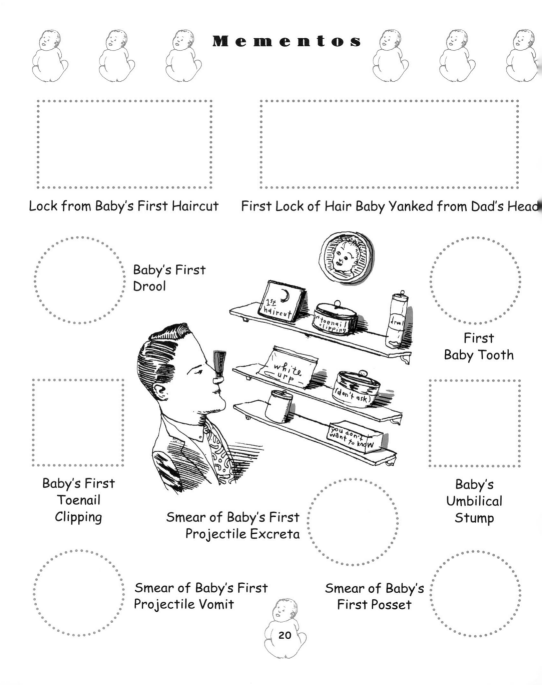

Lock from Baby's First Haircut

First Lock of Hair Baby Yanked from Dad's Head

Baby's First Drool

First Baby Tooth

Baby's First Toenail Clipping

Smear of Baby's First Projectile Excreta

Baby's Umbilical Stump

Smear of Baby's First Projectile Vomit

Smear of Baby's First Posset

# Baby's First Nappy

Most Dirty Nappies in a Day . . . . . . . . . . . . . . . . . . . . . . . . . . . . . . . . . . . .

Who Does 99.9% of the Changing . . . . . . . . . . . . . . . . . . . . . . . . . . . . . .

Number of Nappies That Officially Fit into a Nappy Wrapper™ . . . .

Number Parents Have Managed to Fit . . . . . . . . . . . . . . . . . . . . . . . . . .

Nicest Place Parents Have Changed a Nappy . . . . . . . . . . . . . . . . . . . . .

Worst Place Parents Have Hidden a Nappy . . . . . . . . . . . . . . . . . . . . . . .

Average Number of Seconds Before Baby Soils a Brand-New Nappy . . .

Number of Times Baby Peed on Dad Before Work . . . . . . . . . . . . . . . .

21

# Baby's First Locomotion

## *Action*

Held Head Up. . . . . . . . . . . . . . . . .

Rolled Over. . . . . . . . . . . . . . . . . .

Crawled . . . . . . . . . . . . . . . . . . . .

Sat Up . . . . . . . . . . . . . . . . . . . . .

Walked. . . . . . . . . . . . . . . . . . . . . . . . . . . . . . . . . . . . . . . .

## *Reaction*

First Fall . . . . . . . . . . . . . . . . . . . . .

First "Ow". . . . . . . . . . . . . . . . . . . .

First Bellyflop . . . . . . . . . . . . . . .

First Stumble . . . . . . . . . . . . . . .

*Baby's First Locomotion*

How Your Parents Met

Internet Chat Room . . . . . . . . . . . . . . . . . . . . . . . . . . . . . . . . . . . . . . .

Biker Bar . . . . . . . . . . . . . . . . . . . . . . . . . . . . . . . . . . . . . . . . . . . . . . . .

Bar/University/Office Party . . . . . . . . . . . . . . . . . . . . . . . . . . . . . . . . .

What Dad Was Drinking . . . . . . . . . . . . . . . . . . . . . . . . . . . . . . . . . . . .

How Many Dad Had . . . . . . . . . . . . . . . . . . . . . . . . . . . . . . . . . . . . . . . .

What Mum Was Drinking . . . . . . . . . . . . . . . . . . . . . . . . . . . . . . . . . . . .

How Many Mum Had . . . . . . . . . . . . . . . . . . . . . . . . . . . . . . . . . . . . . . .

Their Song . . . . . . . . . . . . . . . . . . . . . . . . . . . . . . . . . . . . . . . . . . . . . . .

Day They Got Married . . . . . . . . . . . . . . . . . . . . . . . . . . . . . . . . . . . . . .

Day Baby Was Born . . . . . . . . . . . . . . . . . . . . . . . . . . . . . . . . . . . . . . . .

Making Baby "Officially" Premature by . . . . . . . . . . . . . Days/Months

# Baby's Family Tree

Mother . . . . . . . . . . . . . . . . . . . . . . . . . . . . . . . . . . . . . . . . . . . .

Birth Mother . . . . . . . . . . . . . . . . . . . . . . . . . . . . . . . . . . . . . . .

Egg Donor . . . . . . . . . . . . . . . . . . . . . . . . . . . . . . . . . . . . . . . . . .

Father . . . . . . . . . . . . . . . . . . . . . . . . . . . . . . . . . . . . . . . . . . . . . .

Biological Father . . . . . . . . . . . . . . . . . . . . . . . . . . . . . . . . . . . . .

Sperm Donor (if known) . . . . . . . . . . . . . . . . . . . . . . . . . . . . . . .

Special Situations:

Other Mummy's Name . . . . . . . . . . . . . . . . . . . . . . . . . . . . . . . .

Daddy's Special Friend . . . . . . . . . . . . . . . . . . . . . . . . . . . . . . . .

Birth Mother's Lawyer's Name . . . . . . . . . . . . . . . . . . . . . . . . . .

Length of Custody Battle . . . . . . . . . . . . . . . . . . . . . . . . . . . . . . .

Cost of Custody Battle . . . . . . . . . . . . . . . . . . . . . . . . . . . . . . . . .

Court Ordered Visitation Rights and/or Restraining Orders . . . . . . . . . . .

Media Spokesperson, Mother's Side . . . . . . . . . . . . . . . . . . . . . . .

Media Spokesperson, Father's Side . . . . . . . . . . . . . . . . . . . . . . .

Media Spokesperson, Birth Mother's Side . . . . . . . . . . . . . . . . . .

Media Spokesperson, Grandparents' Side . . . . . . . . . . . . . . . . . .

# T V  S h o w s  B a b y ' s
# A p p e a r e d  O n

*Kilroy* . . . . . . . . . . . . . . . . . . . . . .  Date/s . . . . . . . . . . . . . . . . . . . . . .

*Jerry Springer* . . . . . . . . . . . . . .  Date/s . . . . . . . . . . . . . . . . . . . . . .

*Trisha* . . . . . . . . . . . . . . . . . . . .  Date/s . . . . . . . . . . . . . . . . . . . . . .

*Oprah* . . . . . . . . . . . . . . . . . . . . .  Date/s . . . . . . . . . . . . . . . . . . . . . .

*Richard and Judy* . . . . . . . . . . . .  Date/s . . . . . . . . . . . . . . . . . . . . . .

*Blind Date* . . . . . . . . . . . . . . . . . .  Date/s . . . . . . . . . . . . . . . . . . . . . .

*Crimewatch* . . . . . . . . . . . . . . . . .  Date/s . . . . . . . . . . . . . . . . . . . . . .

*GMTV* . . . . . . . . . . . . . . . . . . . . .  Date/s . . . . . . . . . . . . . . . . . . . . . .

*Pop Idol* . . . . . . . . . . . . . . . . . . .  Date/s . . . . . . . . . . . . . . . . . . . . . .

*Ibiza Uncovered* . . . . . . . . . . . . . .  Date/s . . . . . . . . . . . . . . . . . . . . . .

*Police, Camera, Action!* . . . . . . . .  Date/s . . . . . . . . . . . . . . . . . . . . . .

*Big Brother* . . . . . . . . . . . . . . . . .  Date/s . . . . . . . . . . . . . . . . . . . . . .

*Ready Steady Cook* . . . . . . . . . . .  Date/s . . . . . . . . . . . . . . . . . . . . . .

TV Shows You've Appeared on

# Siblings

Brothers . . . . . . . . . . . . . . . . . . . . . . . . . . . . . . . . . . . . . . . . . . . . . . . . . . . . . . .

. . . . . . . . . . . . . . . . . . . . . . . . . . . . . . . . . . . . . . . . . . . . . . . . . . . . . . . . .

Sisters . . . . . . . . . . . . . . . . . . . . . . . . . . . . . . . . . . . . . . . . . . . . . . . . . . . . . . .

. . . . . . . . . . . . . . . . . . . . . . . . . . . . . . . . . . . . . . . . . . . . . . . . . . . . . . . . .

Stepbrothers . . . . . . . . . . . . . . . . .  Visitation Rights . . . . . . . . . . . . .

. . . . . . . . . . . . . . . . . . . . . . . . . . . . . . . . . . . . . . . . . . . . . . . . . . . . . . . . .

Stepsisters . . . . . . . . . . . . . . . . . .  Visitation Rights . . . . . . . . . . . . .

. . . . . . . . . . . . . . . . . . . . . . . . . . . . . . . . . . . . . . . . . . . . . . . . . . . . . . . . .

Half-Brothers . . . . . . . . . . . . . . . . .  Visitation Rights . . . . . . . . . . . . .

. . . . . . . . . . . . . . . . . . . . . . . . . . . . . . . . . . . . . . . . . . . . . . . . . . . . . . . . .

Half-Sisters . . . . . . . . . . . . . . . . . .  Visitation Rights . . . . . . . . . . . . .

. . . . . . . . . . . . . . . . . . . . . . . . . . . . . . . . . . . . . . . . . . . . . . . . . . . . . . . . .

"Weird" Uncles . . . . . . . . . . . . . . . . .  Length of Parole . . . . . . . . . . . . .

. . . . . . . . . . . . . . . . . . . . . . . . . . . . . . . . . . . . . . . . . . . . . . . . . . . . . . . . .

## Mother's Side

What They Like Baby to Call Them . . . . . . . . . . . & . . . . . . . . . . . . .

How Hurt They Were That Baby Wasn't Named After One of Them

. . . . . . . . . . . . . . . . . . . . . . . . . . . . . . . . . . . . . . . . . . . . . . .

Exactly How They Would Raise Baby Differently . . . . . . . . . . . . . . . .

. . . . . . . . . . . . . . . . . . . . . . . . . . . . . . . . . . . . . . . . . . . . . . .

How Many Times a Day They Tell Parents What They're Doing Wrong

. . . . . . . . . . . . . . . . . . . . . . . . . . . . . . . . . . . . . . . . . . . . . . .

Times They Show Up Each Week Without Calling First . . . . . . . . . . . .

Things They Give Baby That They Never Gave Parents . . . . . . . . . . .

. . . . . . . . . . . . . . . . . . . . . . . . . . . . . . . . . . . . . . . . . . . . . . .

First Time Baby Talked to Granny on the Phone. . . . . . . . . . . . . . . . .

Minutes Baby Said Nothing Even Though We Can't Shut Baby Up

Any Other Time . . . . . . . . . . . . . . . . . . . . . . . . . . . . . . . . . . . . . .

## Father's Side

What They Like Baby to Call Them . . . . . . . . . . . . & . . . . . . . . . . . . .

How Hurt They Were That Baby Wasn't Named After One of Them

. . . . . . . . . . . . . . . . . . . . . . . . . . . . . . . . . . . . . . . . . . . . . . .

# Grandparents

Exactly How They Would Raise Baby Differently . . . . . . . . . . . . . . . . .

. . . . . . . . . . . . . . . . . . . . . . . . . . . . . . . . . . . . . . . . . . . . . . . . . .

How Many Times a Day They Tell Parents What They're Doing Wrong

. . . . . . . . . . . . . . . . . . . . . . . . . . . . . . . . . . . . . . . . . . . . . . . . . .

Times They Show Up Each Week Without Calling First . . . . . . . . . . . .

Things They Give Baby That They Never Gave Parents . . . . . . . . . . . .

. . . . . . . . . . . . . . . . . . . . . . . . . . . . . . . . . . . . . . . . . . . . . . . . . .

First Time Baby Talked to Granny on the Phone . . . . . . . . . . . . . . . . .

Minutes Baby Said Nothing Even Though We Can't Shut Baby Up

Any Other Time . . . . . . . . . . . . . . . . . . . . . . . . . . . . . . . . . . . . . . . .

Grandparents

# Special People in Baby's Life

## Stepfather

Number of Children Living with His First Wife . . . . . . . . . . . . . . . . . .

Monthly Child Support . . . . . . . .    Months He's Usually Behind. . . . . .

What He Wants Baby to Call Him . . . . . . . . . . . . . . . . . . . . . . . . . . . . .

## Stepfather's Family

Ex-Wife's Name. . . . . . . . . . . . .    Reason She Left Him . . . . . . . . . . .

Difference Between the Way He Treats Baby and the Way He

Treats His Own Kids. . . . . . . . . . . . . . . . . . . . . . . . . . . . . . . . . . . . . . .

## Stepmother

Ex-Husband's Name . . . . . . . . . .  Reason He Left Her . . . . . . . . . . . . .

What She Wants Baby to Call Her . . . . . . . . . . . . . . . . . . . . . . . . . . . .

Difference Between the Way She Treats Baby and the Way She

Treats Her Own Kids . . . . . . . . . . . . . . . . . . . . . . . . . . . . . . . . . . . . . .

## Stepgrandparents

Court-Ordered Visitation Days . . . . . . . . . . . . . . . . . . . . . . . . . . . . . . .

How Much It Cost Them to Get Those. . . . . . . . . . . . . . . . . . . . . . . . . .

Years Court Battle Lasted. . . . . . . . . . . . . . . . . . . . . . . . . . . . . . . . . . .

Mother

Egg Donor

Birth Mother

Mummy's
Special
Friend

Babysitter

Family
Tree

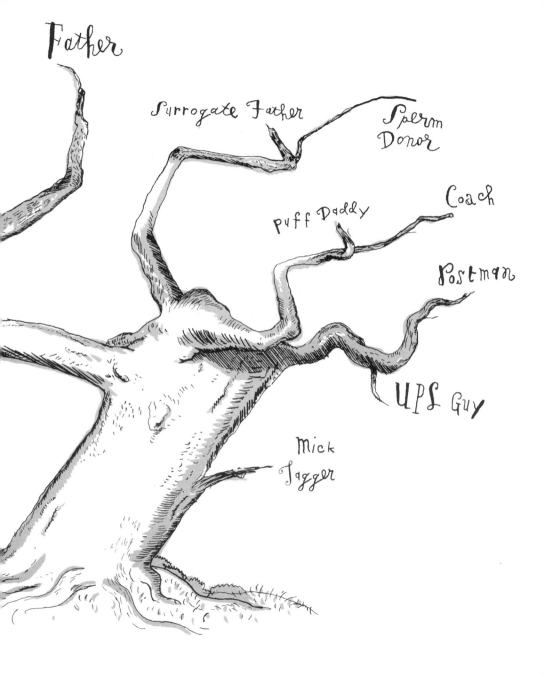

# Disciplining the Problem Grandparents

Times you've had to tell them that a £150 antique porcelain doll is not an appropriate gift for a baby. . . . . . . . . . . . . . . . . . . . . . . . . . . . . . .

Times you've had to say, "Please don't say, 'She's dressed like a ragamuffin,' " in front of the child. . . . . . . . . . . . . . . . . . . . . . . . . . . . . . .

Times you've had to tell them, "Thanks for the clothes, but could you get something that doesn't have to be dry-cleaned next time?"

. . . . . . . . . . . . . . . . . . . . . . . . . . . . . . . . . . . . . . . . . . . . . . . . . . . . . . .

Times you've had to tell them, "Thanks for the clothes, but could you get something that doesn't have to be ironed next time?"

. . . . . . . . . . . . . . . . . . . . . . . . . . . . . . . . . . . . . . . . . . . . . . . . . . . . . . .

Times you've had to tell them, "Thanks for the clothes, but could you get something that isn't white next time?" . . . . . . . . . . . . . . . . . .

Times you've had to tell them, "Thanks for the clothes, but could you get something that doesn't have tiny buttons my child will choke on next time?" . . . . . . . . . . . . . . . . . . . . . . . . . . . . . . . . . . . .

Times you've said, "She's two months old and you bought her a thong?". . . . . . . . . . . . . . . . . . . . . . . . . . . . . . . . . . . . . . . . . . . . .

# Wildly Inappropriate Gifts Grandparents Are Not Allowed to Bring into the House

*Little Black Sambo* Books

Baby's First Shotgun

WWF Action Figures

Home Beer-Brewing Kit

Candy Cigarettes

Jar Jar Binks Doll

Hooters Barbie

Chewing Tobacco

Baby's First Bridge Cards

Baby's First ATM Card

Baby's First Filofax

Disciplining the Problem Grandparent

# Baby's Sleep

Where Baby Sleeps. . . . . . . . . . . . . . . . . . . . . . . . . . . . . . . . . . . . . . . . .

Hours Baby Slept the First Night (if any). . . . . . . . . . . . . . . . . . . . . . . .

Hours Baby Slept the Second Night (if any). . . . . . . . . . . . . . . . . . . . . .

First Time Baby Slept All Night (include year). . . . . . . . . . . . . . . . . . . .

Length of Time Your Father Would Let Baby Cry If I Let Him

. . . . . . . . . . . . . . . . . . . . . . . . . . . . . . . . . . . . . . . . . . . . . . . . . . . . . . . . . . . .

First Time Baby Cried All Night

. . . . . . . . . . . . . . . . . . . . . . . . . . . . . . . .

First Time Baby Screamed All Night

. . . . . . . . . . . . . . . . . . . . . . . . . . . . . . . .

First Night-Terror Episode

. . . . . . . . . . . . . . . . . . . . . . . . . . . . . . . .

Baby's Stated Bedtime

. . . . . . . . . . . . . . . . . . . . . . . . . . . . . . . .

Baby's Real Bedtime

. . . . . . . . . . . . . . . . . . . . . . . . . . . . . . . .

Parents' Sleep

# Parents' Sleep

Hours the First Week . . . . . . . . . . . . . . . . . . . . . . . . . . . . . . . . . . . . . .

Hours the Second Week . . . . . . . . . . . . . . . . . . . . . . . . . . . . . . . . . . . . .

Hours the Third Week . . . . . . . . . . . . . . . . . . . . . . . . . . . . . . . . . . . . . . .


Parents First Fight over Ferberism . . . . . . . . . . . . . . . . . . . . . . . . . . . .

Parents Second Fight over Ferberism . . . . . . . . . . . . . . . . . . . . . . . . . . .

Parents First Fight with Other Parents over Ferberism . . . . . . . . . . .

First Night Dad Leaves the Family Bed to Sleep on the Sofa

. . . . . . . . . . . . . . . . . . . . . . . . . . . . . . . . . . . . . . . . . . . . . . . . . . . . . . . .

Mum's First Sign of Sleep Deprivation . . . . . . . . . . . . . . . . . . . . . . . . .

Mum's First Attempt at Self-Medication . . . . . . . . . . . . . . . . . . . . . . .

Mum's First Valium Prescription . . . . . . . . . . . . . . . . . . . . . . . . . . . . . .

Mum's First Talk With Dad About Getting a Nanny . . . . . . . . . . . . . . .

First Nanny's Name . . . . . . . . . . . . . . . . . . . . . . . . . . . . . . . . . . . . . . . .

Nanny's First Sign of Sleep Deprivation . . . . . . . . . . . . . . . . . . . . . . . .

Nanny's First Attempt at Self-Medication . . . . . . . . . . . . . . . . . . . . . .

Second Nanny's Name . . . . . . . . . . . . . . . . . . . . . . . . . . . . . . . . . . . . . .

First Nanny's Lawyer's Name . . . . . . . . . . . . . . . . . . . . . . . . . . . . . . . .

# How Long It Took Baby to Figure Out How to Get Out of

Crib. . . . . . . . . . . . . . . . . . . . . . . . . . . . . . . . . . . . . . . . . . . . . . . . . . . . . . . . . . . .

Highchair. . . . . . . . . . . . . . . . . . . . . . . . . . . . . . . . . . . . . . . . . . . . . . . . . . . . . . .

Baby Swing . . . . . . . . . . . . . . . . . . . . . . . . . . . . . . . . . . . . . . . . . . . . . . . . . . . . .

Playpen. . . . . . . . . . . . . . . . . . . . . . . . . . . . . . . . . . . . . . . . . . . . . . . . . . . . . . . . . .

Bouncy Chair. . . . . . . . . . . . . . . . . . . . . . . . . . . . . . . . . . . . . . . . . . . . . . . . . . . . .

Stroller . . . . . . . . . . . . . . . . . . . . . .

Car Seat . . . . . . . . . . . . . . . .

How long it took baby to figure out
how to get out of highchair

How Far Baby Can Crawl When Parents Are Watching . . . . . . . . . . . . . .

. . . . . . . . . . . . . . . . . . . . . . . . . . . . . . . . . . . . . . . . . . . . . . . . . . . . .

How Far Baby Can Crawl When Parents Turn Their Heads for Half

a Second . . . . . . . . . . . . . . . . . . . . . . . . . . . . . . . . . . . . . . . . . . . .

. . . . . . . . . . . . . . . . . . . . . . . . . . . . . . . . . . . . . . . . . . . . . . . . . . . . .

Places Baby Crawls That Parents Didn't Think Possible . . . . . . . . . . . .

. . . . . . . . . . . . . . . . . . . . . . . . . . . . . . . . . . . . . . . . . . . . . . . . . . . . .

Cause of Baby's First Scab/Bruise . . . . . . . . . . . . . . . . . . . . . . . . .

. . . . . . . . . . . . . . . . . . . . . . . . . . . . . . . . . . . . . . . . . . . . . . . . . . . . .

Funny Looks People Give Parents in the Supermarket When

They See It . . . . . . . . . . . . . . . . . . . . . . . . . . . . . . . . . . . . . . . . . .

How Parents Laugh It Off When People Ask About Baby's

Scab/Bruise . . . . . . . . . . . . . . . . . . . . . . . . . . . . . . . . . . . . . . . . .

Hours Parents Wonder if They Believed It or Not . . . . . . . . . . . . . .

Most Disgusting Thing Baby Has Ever Put in Its Mouth . . . . . . . . . . .

. . . . . . . . . . . . . . . . . . . . . . . . . . . . . . . . . . . . . . . . . . . . . . . . . . . . .

Most Disgusting Thing Parents Have Ever Put in Their Mouths

. . . . . . . . . . . . . . . . . . . . . . . . . . . . . . . . . . . . . . . . . . . . . . . . . . . . .

# Last Time Mum and Dad Had Sex

Can't Remember Day . . . . . . . . . . . . . . . . . . . . . . . . . . . . . . . . . . . . . . . . . .

Can't Remember Month . . . . . . . . . . . . . . . . . . . . . . . . . . . . . . . . . . . . . . . . .

Can't Remember Year . . . . . . . . . . . . . . . . . . . . . . . . . . . . . . . . . . . . . . . . . . .

The last time Mum and Dad had sex

Restaurants We Never Go to Any More . . . . . . . . . . . . . . . . . . . . . . . . . .

. . . . . . . . . . . . . . . . . . . . . . . . . . . . . . . . . . . . . . . . . . . . . . . . . . . . . . . .

. . . . . . . . . . . . . . . . . . . . . . . . . . . . . . . . . . . . . . . . . . . . . . . . . . . . . . . .

Places We've Been Asked to Leave . . . . . . . . . . . . . . . . . . . . . . . . . . .

. . . . . . . . . . . . . . . . . . . . . . . . . . . . . . . . . . . . . . . . . . . . . . . . . . . . . . . .

. . . . . . . . . . . . . . . . . . . . . . . . . . . . . . . . . . . . . . . . . . . . . . . . . . . . . . . .

Child-Free Friends We Never See Any More . . . . . . . . . . . . . . . . . . . .

. . . . . . . . . . . . . . . . . . . . . . . . . . . . . . . . . . . . . . . . . . . . . . . . . . . . . . . .

. . . . . . . . . . . . . . . . . . . . . . . . . . . . . . . . . . . . . . . . . . . . . . . . . . . . . . . .

Oscar-Winning Movies We've Never Seen . . . . . . . . . . . . . . . . . . . . .

. . . . . . . . . . . . . . . . . . . . . . . . . . . . . . . . . . . . . . . . . . . . . . . . . . . . . . . .

. . . . . . . . . . . . . . . . . . . . . . . . . . . . . . . . . . . . . . . . . . . . . . . . . . . . . . . .

Overseas Places We'll Never See . . . . . . . . . . . . . . . . . . . . . . . . . . . .

. . . . . . . . . . . . . . . . . . . . . . . . . . . . . . . . . . . . . . . . . . . . . . . . . . . . . . . .

. . . . . . . . . . . . . . . . . . . . . . . . . . . . . . . . . . . . . . . . . . . . . . . . . . . . . . . .

First Neighbour to Move Away . . . . . . . . . . . . . . . . . . . . . . . . . . . . . .

# Breast-Feeding

What Mum's Closest Relatives Think About It. . . . . . . . . . . . . . . . . . .

. . . . . . . . . . . . . . . . . . . . . . . . . . . . . . . . . . . . . . . . . . . . . . . . . . . . .

How Often They Tell Mum What They Think About It . . . . . . . . . . .

. . . . . . . . . . . . . . . . . . . . . . . . . . . . . . . . . . . . . . . . . . . . . . . . . . . . .

The Last Time Daddy Showed Interest in Breasts . . . . . . . . . . . . . .

. . . . . . . . . . . . . . . . . . . . . . . . . . . . . . . . . . . . . . . . . . . . . . . . . . . . .

First Time Baby Suckled Dad's Nipple by Mistake. . . . . . . . . . . . . .

. . . . . . . . . . . . . . . . . . . . . . . . . . . . . . . . . . . . . . . . . . . . . . . . . . . . .

How High He Jumped . . . . . . . . . . . . . . . . . . . . . . . . . . . . . . . . . . . .

How Loud He Screamed . . . . . . . . . . . . . . . . . . . . . . . . . . . . . . . . . .

How Mum Labels Your Breast Milk in the Office Fridge . . . . . . . . . .

. . . . . . . . . . . . . . . . . . . . . . . . . . . . . . . . . . . . . . . . . . . . . . . . . . . . .

Name of Guy Who Used It in His Coffee. . . . . . . . . . . . . . . . . . . . . .

How Much He Puked When Mum Told Him What It Was . . . . . . . . . .

. . . . . . . . . . . . . . . . . . . . . . . . . . . . . . . . . . . . . . . . . . . . . . . . . . . . .

# Baby's Favourite Food

Apple Sauce with Mashed Banana . . .

Peaches with Mashed Banana . . . . . .

Spinach with Mashed Banana . . . . . . .

Puréed Carrot with Mashed Banana .

Mashed Banana with Mashed Banana

*Baby's Favourite Food*

Most Parents Ever Paid for a 100g Serving of Mashed Banana . . . . . .

. . . . . . . . . . . . . . . . . . . . . . . . . . . . . . . . . . . . . . . . . . . . . . .

Baby's First Picky-Eating Incident . . . . . . . . . . . . . . . . . . . . . . . . . . . .

Formerly Favourite Food Baby Suddenly Decided Not to Eat . . . . . . .

. . . . . . . . . . . . . . . . . . . . . . . . . . . . . . . . . . . . . . . . . . . . . . .

First Time Baby Ate Dirt . . . . . . . . . . . . . . . . . . . . . . . . . . . . . . . . . .

How Quickly We Got Baby to A&E Afterwards . . . . . . . . . . . . . . . . . .

. . . . . . . . . . . . . . . . . . . . . . . . . . . . . . . . . . . . . . . . . . . . . . .

How Many Times a Week Baby Eats Dirt Now . . . . . . . . . . . . . . . . . . .

How Much Dirt Costs . . . . . . . . . . . . . . . . . . . . . . . . . . . . . . . . . . . .

# Baby's First Web Page

URL . . . . . . . . . . . . . . . . . . . . @ . . . . . . . . . . . . . . . . . . . . . . .co.uk

Length of Videotape of Birth on Streaming Video. . . . . . . . . . . . . . . .

Baby's First Email Address . . . . . . . . . . . . . . . . . @ . . . . . . . . . . . . . .

Baby's First Chat-Room Handle . . . . . . . . . . . . . . . . . . . . . . . . . . . . . .


Baby's First Video Game . . . . . . . . . . . . . . . . . . . . . . . . . . . . . . . . . . .

First Time Baby Created Internet Virus . . . . . . . . . . . . . . . . . . . . . . . .

First Inappropriate Website Baby Visited . . . . . . . . . . . . . . . . . . . . . . .

First Time Baby Overrode Parental Controls . . . . . . . . . . . . . . . . . . . .

# Pictures...

## That Are Only Here to Embarrass Baby at Their Eighteenth Birthday Party, Perhaps Emotionally Scarring the Child Forever

43

Baby's First Bath . . . . . . . . . . . . . . . . . . . . .

First Time Baby Rolled Over by Itself . . . . .

. . . . . . . . . . . . . . . . . . . . . . . . . . . . . .

First Time Baby Crawled . . . . . . . . . . . . . .

Stuff Parents Put in Storage Because

Baby Started Crawling . . . . . . . . . . . . . . . . .

. . . . . . . . . . . . . . . . . . . . . . . . . . . . . .

First Time Baby Pulled Itself Up . . . . . . . . . . . . . . . . . . . . . . . . . . . . . . . .

First Time Baby Reached for Object . . . . . . . . . . . . . . . . . . . . . . . . . . . . .

First Time Baby Broke an Irreplaceable Heirloom . . . . . . . . . . . . . . . . .

Baby's First Drink from a Bottle . . . . . . . . . . . . . . . . . . . . . . . . . . . . . . .

Baby's First Burp . . . . . . . . . . . . . . . . . . . . . . . . . . . . . . . . . . . . . . . . . .

Clothes Ruined . . . . . . . . . . .

. . . . . . . . . . . . . . . . . . . . . . . .

. . . . . . . . . . . . . . . . . . . . . . . .

*First Bath*

*First time Baby crawled*

Baby's First Solid Food . . .

. . . . . . . . . . . . . . . . . . . . . .

First Spitting Up Solid Food

. . . . . . . . . . . . . . . . . . . . . .

Baby's First Meal . . . . . . . .

. . . . . . . . . . . . . . . . . . . . . .

First Meal Cleanup . . . . . . . . . . . . . . . . . . . . . . . . . . . . . .

First Time Baby Stood Up . . . . . . . . . . . . . . . . . . . . . . . . . .

Baby's First Tooth . . . . . . . . . . . . . . . . . . . . . . . . . . . . . .

Baby's First Dentist Appointment . . . . . . . . . . . . . .

Baby's First Step . . . . . . . . . . . . . . . . . . . . . . . .

Baby's First Pair of £50 Shoes . . . . . . . . . . . . .

    Times Worn . . . . . . . . . . . . . . . . . . . . . . . .

Baby's First Haircut . . . . . . . . . . . . . . . . . . . . . . .

Baby's First Santa Visit . . . . . . . . . . . . . . . . . . . .

Baby's First Birthday . . . . . . . . . . . . . . . . . . . . . .

First Time Baby Cried Because Batteries Weren't Included . . . . . . .

. . . . . . . . . . . . . . . . . . . . . . . . . . . . . . . . . . . . . . . . . . .

First Spitting Up Solid Food

First Haircut

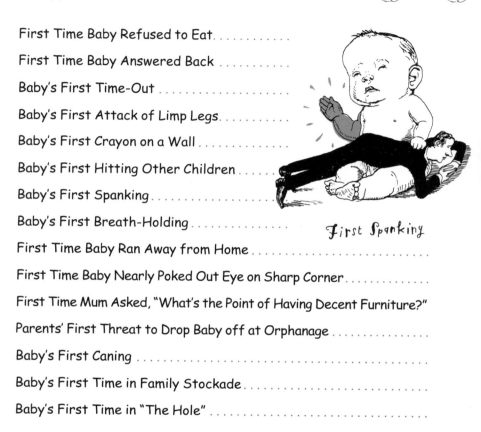

First Time Baby Refused to Eat . . . . . . . . . . .

First Time Baby Answered Back . . . . . . . . . . .

Baby's First Time-Out . . . . . . . . . . . . . . . . .

Baby's First Attack of Limp Legs . . . . . . . . . . .

Baby's First Crayon on a Wall . . . . . . . . . . . . .

Baby's First Hitting Other Children . . . . . .

Baby's First Spanking . . . . . . . . . . . . . . . . . .

Baby's First Breath-Holding . . . . . . . . . . . . . .

*First Spanking*

First Time Baby Ran Away from Home . . . . . . . . . . . . . . . . . . . . . . . . . . .

First Time Baby Nearly Poked Out Eye on Sharp Corner . . . . . . . . . . . . . .

First Time Mum Asked, "What's the Point of Having Decent Furniture?"

Parents' First Threat to Drop Baby off at Orphanage . . . . . . . . . . . . . . . .

Baby's First Caning . . . . . . . . . . . . . . . . . . . . . . . . . . . . . . . . . . . . . . . .

Baby's First Time in Family Stockade . . . . . . . . . . . . . . . . . . . . . . . . . . . .

Baby's First Time in "The Hole" . . . . . . . . . . . . . . . . . . . . . . . . . . . . . . . .

# First Trip to Granny and Grandpa's

Miles Away They Live . . . . . . . . . . . . . . . . . . . . . . . . . . . . . . . . . . . . . . . . .

Hours it Takes to Get There . . . . . . . . . . . . . . . . . . . . . . . . . . . . . . . . . .

The One Thing in the Entire World That Keeps Baby from Crying

. . . . . . . . . . . . . . . . . . . . . . . . . . . . . . . . . . . . . . . . . . . . . . . . . . . . . . . . . .

Who Forgot to Pack It . . . . . . . . . . . . . . . . . . . . . . . . . . . . . . . . . . . . . . . . .

Hours Baby Screamed While the Plane Sat on the Runway . . . . . . . . .

. . . . . . . . . . . . . . . . . . . . . . . . . . . . . . . . . . . . . . . . . . . . . . . . . . . . . . . . . .

First Nappy Changed on Plane . . . . . . . . . . . . . . . . . . . . . . . . . . . . . . . . .

Name of First Passenger to Complain . . . . . . . . . . . . . . . . . . . . . . . . . . .

How Many Seconds After Flight Landed Baby Stopped Crying . . . . .

. . . . . . . . . . . . . . . . . . . . . . . . . . . . . . . . . . . . . . . . . . . . . . . . . . . . . . . . . .

Number of People Who Gave Parents Dirty Looks . . . . . . . . . . . . . . . .

. . . . . . . . . . . . . . . . . . . . . . . . . . . . . . . . . . . . . . . . . . . . . . . . . . . . . . . . . .

# The Stuff We Have to Carry with Us Every Single Goddamn Place We Go Checklist

- ☐ Car Seat
- ☐ Stroller
- ☐ Nappy Bag
- ☐ Dirty-Nappy Bag
- ☐ Dummies
- ☐ Rattles
- ☐ Bottles
- ☐ Juice
- ☐ Milk
- ☐ Medicine
- ☐ Teething Rings
- ☐ Wet Wipes
- ☐ Spare Clothes
- ☐ Favourite Blankie
- ☐ Bibs
- ☐ Baby Spoons
- ☐ Training Cup

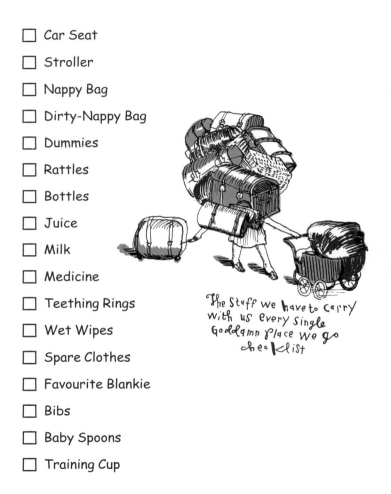

The Stuff we have to carry with us every single Goddamn place we go checklist

48

# The Stuff We Forget to Carry with Us Every Single Goddamn Place We Go Checklist

- ☐ Car Seat
- ☐ Stroller
- ☐ Nappy Bag
- ☐ Dirty-Nappy Bag
- ☐ Dummies
- ☐ Rattles
- ☐ Bottles
- ☐ Juice
- ☐ Milk
- ☐ Medicine
- ☐ Teething Rings
- ☐ Wet Wipes
- ☐ Spare Clothes
- ☐ Favourite Blankie
- ☐ Bibs
- ☐ Baby Spoons
- ☐ Training Cup

# Baby's First Words

Baby's First Word . . . . . . . . . . . . . . . . . . . . . . . . . . . . . . . . . . . . . . . . . . .

First Day Baby Says "Mama" . . . . . . . . . . . . . . . . . . . . . . . . . . . . . . . . . . . .

First Day Baby Says "Dada" . . . . . . . . . . . . . . . . . . . . . . . . . . . . . . . . . . . .

Baby's First Four-Letter Word . . . . . . . . . . . . . . . . . . . . . . . . . . . . . . . . .

Public Place We Were in When It Was Spoken . . . . . . . . . . . . . . . . . . .

First Time Parents Said "No" . . . . . . . . . . . . . . . . . . . . . . . . . . . . . . . . . .

First Time Parents Said "Don't Touch" . . . . . . . . . . . . . . . . . . . . . . . . .

First Person to Ask Parents to Stop Bringing Baby to Visit

. . . . . . . . . . . . . . . . . . . . . . . . . . . . . . . . . . . . . . . . . . . . . . . . . . . . . . . . .

Baby's First Words

50

# Baby's First Babysitter

Her Name . . . . . . . . . . . . . . . . . . . . . . . . . . . . . . . . . . . . . . . . . . . . . . . . . . .

Her Age . . . . . . . . . . . . . . . . . . . . . . . . . . . . . . . . . . . . . . . . . . . . . . . . . . . . .

Hours Parents Left Her Alone with Baby . . . . . . . . . . . . . . . . . . . . . . . . . . .

How Much Parents Paid Her per Hour . . . . . . . . . . . . . . . . . . . . . . . . . . . . . .

Hours It Took Dad to Drive Her Home . . . . . . . . . . . . . . . . . . . . . . . . . . . . . .

Yards Away She Lives . . . . . . . . . . . . . . . . . . . . . . . . . . . . . . . . . . . . . . . . . . . .

Length of Argument When Dad Got Back . . . . . . . . . . . . . . . . . . . . . . . . . .

Babysitter's First Lawyer . . . . . . . . . . . . . . . . . . . . . . . . . . . . . . . . . . . . . . . .

# Baby's Childhood Diseases

Threadworm . . . . . . . . . . . . . . . . . . . . .    Date/s . . . . . . . . . . . . . . . . . . . . . . . . . . . .

Head Lice . . . . . . . . . . . . . . . . . . .    Date/s . . . . . . . . . . . . . . . . . . . . . . . . . . . .

Earache . . . . . . . . . . . . . . . . . . . . . .    Date/s . . . . . . . . . . . . . . . . . . . . . . . . . . . .

Diarrhoea . . . . . . . . . . . . . . . . . . .    Date/s . . . . . . . . . . . . . . . . . . . . . . . . . . . .

Chickenpox . . . . . . . . . . . . . . . . . .    Date . . . . . . . . . . . . . . . . . . . . . . . . . . . . . .

Diphtheria . . . . . . . . . . . . . . . .    Date . . . . . . . . . . . . . . . . . . . . . . . . . . . . . .

Mumps . . . . . . . . . . . . . . . . . . . . . .    Date . . . . . . . . . . . . . . . . . . . . . . . . . . . . . .

Whooping Cough . . . . . . . . . . . . . .    Date/s . . . . . . . . . . . . . . . . . . . . . . . . . . . .

Asthma Attack . . . . . . . . . . . . . . .    Date/s . . . . . . . . . . . . . . . . . . . . . . . . . . . .

Bronchitis . . . . . . . . . . . . . . . . . .    Date/s . . . . . . . . . . . . . . . . . . . . . . . . . . . .

Pneumonia . . . . . . . . . . . . . . . . . .    Date/s . . . . . . . . . . . . . . . . . . . . . . . . . . . .

Impetigo . . . . . . . . . . . . . . . . . . .    Date/s . . . . . . . . . . . . . . . . . . . . . . . . . . . .

Cradle Cap . . . . . . . . . . . . . . . . . .    Date/s . . . . . . . . . . . . . . . . . . . . . . . . . . . .

Eczema . . . . . . . . . . . . . . . . . . . . .  Date/s . . . . . . . . . . . . . . . . . . . . . . . . . . .

Croup . . . . . . . . . . . . . . . . . . . . . .  Date/s . . . . . . . . . . . . . . . . . . . . . . . . . . .

Jaundice . . . . . . . . . . . . . . . . . . . .  Date/s . . . . . . . . . . . . . . . . . . . . . . . . . . .

Lead Poisoning . . . . . . . . . . . . . . .  Date/s . . . . . . . . . . . . . . . . . . . . . . . . . . .

Depression . . . . . . . . . . . . . . . . . . .  Date/s . . . . . . . . . . . . . . . . . . . . . . . . . . .

Strep Throat . . . . . . . . . . . . . . . . . .  Date/s . . . . . . . . . . . . . . . . . . . . . . . . . . .

Tonsillitis . . . . . . . . . . . . . . . . . . . .  Date/s . . . . . . . . . . . . . . . . . . . . . . . . . . .

Blocked Bowel . . . . . . . . . . . . . . . .  Date/s . . . . . . . . . . . . . . . . . . . . . . . . . . .

Attention Deficit Disorder . . . . .  Date/s . . . . . . . . . . . . . . . . . . . . . . . . . . .

Cold and 'Flu . . . . . . . . . . . . . . . .  Date/s . . . . . . . . . . . . . . . . . . . . . . . . . . .

Eating Disorders . . . . . . . . . . . . .  Date/s . . . . . . . . . . . . . . . . . . . . . . . . . . .

Substance Abuse . . . . . . . . . . . . .  Date/s . . . . . . . . . . . . . . . . . . . . . . . . . . .

Allergies . . . . . . . . . . . . . . . . . . . .  Date/s . . . . . . . . . . . . . . . . . . . . . . . . . . .

Name . . . . . . . . . Price . . . . . . Colour* . . . . . Bad Reaction . . . . . .

Name . . . . . . . . . Price . . . . . . Colour . . . . . . Bad Reaction . . . . . .

Name . . . . . . . . . Price . . . . . . Colour . . . . . . Bad Reaction . . . . . .

Name . . . . . . . . . Price . . . . . . Colour . . . . . . Bad Reaction . . . . . .

Name . . . . . . . . . Price . . . . . . Colour . . . . . . Bad Reaction . . . . . .

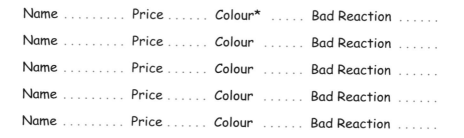

First Trip to A&E. . . . . . . . . . . . . . . . . . . . . . . . . . . . . . . . . . . . . .

Second Trip (if less than 24 hours later) . . . . . . . . . . . . . . . . . . . . . .

Most Trips to A&E in One Day . . . . . . . . . . . . . . . . . . . . . . . . . . . . .

Name of First Doctor Who Didn't Seem to Understand

the Problem . . . . . . . . . . . . . . . . . . . . . . . . . . . . . . . . . . . . . . . . .

Name of Second Doctor Who Didn't Seem to Understand

the Problem . . . . . . . . . . . . . . . . . . . . . . . . . . . . . . . . . . . . . . . . .

Doctor We're Seeing Now. . . . . . . . . . . . . . . . . . . . . . . . . . . . . . . . .

* Colour of stain medicine will leave on expensive baby clothes

# Baby's Life-Threatening, Attention-Getting, Conversation-Monopolizing Allergies

Cow's Milk

Peanuts

All Nuts

Gluten

Corn

Latex

Tree Pollen

Mould Spores

Dust Mites

Cat Hair

Shellfish

Mashed Banana

Soap

Anything Inexpensive

Cost of Education . . . . . . . . . . . . . . . . . . . . . . . . . . . . . . . . . . . . . . .

Primary . . . . . . . . . . . . . . . . . . . . . . . . . . . . . . . . . . . . . . . . . . . . . .

Secondary . . . . . . . . . . . . . . . . . . . . . . . . . . . . . . . . . . . . . . . . . . . .

Extras (Uniforms, Lost Books, Instruments, Sports Equipment,

School Trips) . . . . . . . . . . . . . . . . . . . . . . . . . . . . . . . . . . . . . . . . . .

Clothes and Shoes . . . . . . . . . . . . . . . . . . . . . . . . . . . . . . . . . . . . . .

Brownies/Cubs/Guides/Scouts . . . . . . . . . . . . . . . . . . . . . . . . . . . .

Food . . . . . . . . . . . . . . . . . . . . . . . . . . . . . . . . . . . . . . . . . . . . . . . .

Snacks . . . . . . . . . . . . . . . . . . . . . . . . . . . . . . . . . . . . . . . . . . . . . .

Cable TV . . . . . . . . . . . . . . . . . . . . . . . . . . . . . . . . . . . . . . . . . . . .

Christmas and Birthday Presents . . . . . . . . . . . . . . . . . . . . . . . . . .

Extra Tuition . . . . . . . . . . . . . . . . . . . . . . . . . . . . . . . . . . . . . . . . .

Therapists . . . . . . . . . . . . . . . . . . . . . . . . . . . . . . . . . . . . . . . . . . .

Summer School . . . . . . . . . . . . . . . . . . . . . . . . . . . . . . . . . . . . . . . .

First Car . . . . . . . . . . . . . . . . . . . . . . . . . . . . . . . . . . . . . . . . . . . . .

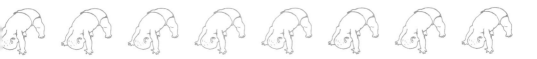

Repairing First Car . . . . . . . . . . . . . . . . . . . . . . . . . . . . . . . . . . . . . . . . . . . .

Auto Insurance . . . . . . . . . . . . . . . . . . . . . . . . . . . . . . . . . . . . . . . . . . . . . . . .

Gap Year . . . . . . . . . . . . . . . . . . . . . . . . . . . . . . . . . . . . . . . . . . . . . . . . . . . . .

University Tours, Travel, etc. . . . . . . . . . . . . . . . . . . . . . . . . . . . . . . . . . . . . .

Help through University . . . . . . . . . . . . . . . . . . . . . . . . . . . . . . . . . . . . . . . . .

Career Counselling. . . . . . . . . . . . . . . . . . . . . . . . . . . . . . . . . . . . . . . . . . . . . .

Post-Grad Education. . . . . . . . . . . . . . . . . . . . . . . . . . . . . . . . . . . . . . . . . . . . .

Cost of Finding Oneself . . . . . . . . . . . . . . . . . . . . . . . . . . . . . . . . . . . . . . . . . .

Miscellaneous . . . . . . . . . . . . . . . . . . . . . . . . . . . . . . . . . . . . . . . . . . . . . . . . . .

. . . . . . . . . . . . . . . . . . . . . . . . . . . . . . . . . . . . . . . . . . . . . . . . . . . . . . . . . . . . . .

. . . . . . . . . . . . . . . . . . . . . . . . . . . . . . . . . . . . . . . . . . . . . . . . . . . . . . . . . . . . . .

Total (in millions) . . . . . . . . . . . . . . . . . . . . . . . . . . . . . . . . . . . . . . . . . . . . . .

# Things Mummy and Daddy Fight About All the Time

Money. . . . . . . . . . . . . . . . . . . . . . . . . . . . . . . . . . . . . . . . . . .

The In-Laws . . . . . . . . . . . . . . . . . . . . . . . . . . . . . . . . . . . . . . .

Nappy Changing . . . . . . . . . . . . . . . . . . . . . . . . . . . . . . . . . . . .

Lack of Sleep . . . . . . . . . . . . . . . . . . . . . . . . . . . . . . . . . . . . . .

Grandparents Dropping In All the Time. . . . . . . . . . . . . . . . . . . . .

Dad's No Help. . . . . . . . . . . . . . . . . . . . . . . . . . . . . . . . . . . . . .

Dad Can Find the Time to Go Drinking with His Friends but Not the

Time to Wash the Dishes . . . . . . . . . . . . . . . . . . . . . . . . . . . . . .

Who Is Not Helping Enough Around the House . . . . . . . . . . . . . . . .

Money. . . . . . . . . . . . . . . . . . . . . . . . . . . . . . . . . . . . . . . . . . .

Lack of Sex. . . . . . . . . . . . . . . . . . . . . . . . . . . . . . . . . . . . . . . .

Money. . . . . . . . . . . . . . . . . . . . . . . . . . . . . . . . . . . . . . . . . . .

# Baby's Potty Training

First Nappy Changed . . . . . . . . . . . . . . . . . . . . . . . . . . . . . . . . . . . .

Last Nappy Changed . . . . . . . . . . . . . . . . . . . . . . . . . . . . . . . . . . . . .

Total Number of Nappies Changed (in thousands) . . . . . . . . . . . . . . . . .

Metric Tons of Baby's Faecal Matter Added to Nearby Landfill

. . . . . . . . . . . . . . . . . . . . . . . . . . . . . . . . . . . . . . . . . . . . . . . . .

Miles in Space Landfill Can Be Seen from . . . . . . . . . . . . . . . . . . . . . . .

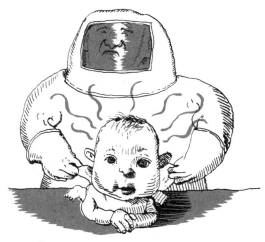

Baby's First Nappy

59

Baby's First Pet

Pet Name . . . . . . . . . . . . . . . . . . . . . . . . . . . . . . . . . . . . . . . . . . . . . . . .

Species (if Known) . . . . . . . . . . . . . . . . . . . . . . . . . . . . . . . . . . . . . . . . .

Breed . . . . . . . . . . . . . . . . . . . . . . . . . . . . . . . . . . . . . . . . . . . . . . . . . . .

Times Baby Begged and Screamed to Have This Pet . . . . . . . . . . . . . . .

First Time Baby Promised to Feed This Pet . . . . . . . . . . . . . . . . . . . . .

. . . . . . . . . . . . . . . . . . . . . . . . . . . . . . . . . . . . . . . . . . . . . . . . . . . . . . .

Times Baby Actually Fed Pet . . . . . . . . . . . . . . . . . . . . . . . . . . . . . . . . .

Cause of Pet's Death (e.g., neglect, starvation, suicide) . . . . . . . . . . .

. . . . . . . . . . . . . . . . . . . . . . . . . . . . . . . . . . . . . . . . . . . . . . . . . . . . . . .

How Many Attended Pet's Moving Burial Service . . . . . . . . . . . . . . . . .

Spot Where Pet Is Buried . . . . . . . . . . . . . . . . . . . . . . . . . . . . . . . . . . . .

Days After Burial Neighbour's Dog Dug It Up . . . . . . . . . . . . . . . . . . . .

# Baby's First Day-Care Centre

Name of Day-Care Centre . . . . . . . . . . . . . . . . . . . . . . . . . . . . . . . . . . . .

Name of Day-Care Centre's Lawyer . . . . . . . . . . . . . . . . . . . . . . . . . . . .

Name of Lawyer Representing Other Parents . . . . . . . . . . . . . . . . . . .

Plaintiff's Witness List . . . . . . . . . . . . . . . . . . . . . . . . . . . . . . . . . . . . . .

Baby's First Lawsuit . . . . . . . . . . . . . . . . . . . . . . . . . . . . . . . . . . . . . . . .

Baby's First Lawyer . . . . . . . . . . . . . . . . . . . . . . . . . . . . . . . . . . . . . . . .

First Presiding Judge . . . . . . . . . . . . . . . . . . . . . . . . . . . . . . . . . . . . . . .

# School Days

Baby's First School . . . . . . . . . . . . . . . . . . . . . . . . . . . . .

Baby's First Day at School . . . . . . . . . . . . . . . . . . . . . . . . . .

Baby's First Teacher's Name . . . . . . . . . . . . . . . . . . . . . . . . .

First Teacher's Meeting . . . . . . . . . . . . . . . . . . . . . . . . . . . .

Date Baby's Teacher Resigned . . . . . . . . . . . . . . . . . . . . . . . . .

Baby's First Ritalin Prescription . . . . . . . . . . . . . . . . . . . . . . .

First Day at Baby's Second School . . . . . . . . . . . . . . . . . . . . . .

First Day at Baby's Third School . . . . . . . . . . . . . . . . . . . . . . .

Baby's First Day of Football/Netball Practice . . . . . . . . . . . . . . . . .

Parents' First Fight with Baby's Coach . . . . . . . . . . . . . . . . . . . . .

Parents' First Fight with Other Parents . . . . . . . . . . . . . . . . . . . .

News Clippings of Fight . . . . . . . . . . . . . . . . . . . . . . . . . . . .

Network News Video of Fight . . . . . . . . . . . . . . . . . . . . . . . . .

First Reason They Gave for Holding Baby Back a Year . . . . . . . . . . . .

Real Reason They Held Baby Back . . . . . . . . . . . . . . . . . . . . . . .

Baby's First Gang . . . . . . . . . . . . . . . . . . . . . . . . . . . . . . . .

Their Colours . . . . . . . . . . . . . . . . . . & . . . . . . . . . . . . . . . .

# Growing Pains

Baby's First Exorcism. . . . . . . . . . . . . . . . . . . . . . . . . . . . . . . . . . . .

Baby's First Tattoo . . . . . . . . . . . . . . . . . . . . . . . . . . . . . . . . . . . . .

Baby's First Body Piercing . . . . . . . . . . . . . . . . . . . . . . . . . . . . . . . .

Baby's First Nose Ring . . . . . . . . . . . . . . . . . . . . . . . . . . . . . . . . . . .

Baby's First Arrest . . . . . . . . . . . . . . . . . . . . . . . . . . . . . . . . . . . . . .

Baby's First Drink-Driving Offence . . . . . . . . . . . . . . . . . . . . . . . . . .

Baby's First Car Written Off . . . . . . . . . . . . . . . . . . . . . . . . . . . . . . .

What Baby's Car Insurance Would Cost if Parents Even Bothered

to Ask. . . . . . . . . . . . . . . . . . . . . . . . . . . . . . . . . . . . . . . . . . . . . . .

# Baby's Big Blue Babysitter

Most Times Baby Ever Watched the Same Video on a Single Day . . . . .

Baby's Favourite Videos . . . . . . . . . . . . . . . . . . . . . . . . . . . . . . . .

. . . . . . . . . . . . . . . . . . . . . . . . . . . . . . . . . . . . . . . . . . . . . . . . . . .

. . . . . . . . . . . . . . . . . . . . . . . . . . . . . . . . . . . . . . . . . . . . . . . . . . .

Videos Baby Likes That Parents Can't Stand . . . . . . . . . . . . . . . . . . .

. . . . . . . . . . . . . . . . . . . . . . . . . . . . . . . . . . . . . . . . . . . . . . . . . . .

. . . . . . . . . . . . . . . . . . . . . . . . . . . . . . . . . . . . . . . . . . . . . . . . . . .

Most Inappropriate Thing Parents Ever Let Baby Watch by Accident

. . . . . . . . . . . . . . . . . . . . . . . . . . . . . . . . . . . . . . . . . . . . . . . . . . .

The Big Blue Baby-sitter

# Messages Baby Gets from Television

Just Ask, Santa Will Get It for You.

Kids on TV Have a Lot More Toys Than You Do.

The Best Restaurants Have Clowns and Play Areas.

Good Parents Take Their Kids to Euro-Disney Almost Every Day.

Mums Don't Wear Dressing-Gowns Until Noon on TV.

Mums and Dads Always Have Time for Their Kids on TV.

Nothing Is Out of Place in the Living Room on TV.

No One Ever Vacuums or Washes Dishes by Hand on TV.

TV Mums Cook the Whole Family a Nutritious Breakfast Every Day.

Those TV Kids Really Are Cute, Not Like You.

No One Ever Cries Eating a Happy Meal.

At Your Age, Tiger Woods Was Already Playing Golf. What's the Matter with You?

If It Doesn't Have the Word "Sugarcoated" on It, It's Not Edible.

Michael Jackson Was Out Supporting His Family at Your Age. Are You Sure You Can't Sing or Dance?

Why Go Outside and Play When the Television's in Here?

# Baby's First Trip to the Shops

Name of Supermarket . . . . . . . . . . . . . . . . . . . . . . . . . . . . . . . . . . . . . . .

First Item Spilled or Broken . . . . . . . . . . . . . . . . . . . . . . . . . . . . . . . . . . .

Baby's First Tantrum in Supermarket . . . . . . . . . . . . . . . . . . . . . . . . . . . .

Number of People Who Said They Would Spank Baby if Parents Didn't

. . . . . . . . . . . . . . . . . . . . . . . . . . . . . . . . . . . . . . . . . . . . . . . . . . . . . . . .

Where Parents Left Trolley Full of Frozen Food When They Had to

Drag Baby Screaming and Yelling out to the Car Park. . . . . . . . . . . . .

. . . . . . . . . . . . . . . . . . . . . . . . . . . . . . . . . . . . . . . . . . . . . . . . . . . . . . . .

First Time Baby's Body Went Limp/Rigid. . . . . . . . . . . . . . . . . . . . . . . . .

First trip to the shops

How Baby First Learned About Sex . . . . . . . . . . . . . . . . . . . . . . . . . . . . .

. . . . . . . . . . . . . . . . . . . . . . . . . . . . . . . . . . . . . . . . . . . . . . . . . . . . . . .

. . . . . . . . . . . . . . . . . . . . . . . . . . . . . . . . . . . . . . . . . . . . . . . . . . . . . . .

. . . . . . . . . . . . . . . . . . . . . . . . . . . . . . . . . . . . . . . . . . . . . . . . . . . . . . .

. . . . . . . . . . . . . . . . . . . . . . . . . . . . . . . . . . . . . . . . . . . . . . . . . . . . . . .

. . . . . . . . . . . . . . . . . . . . . . . . . . . . . . . . . . . . . . . . . . . . . . . . . . . . . . .

. . . . . . . . . . . . . . . . . . . . . . . . . . . . . . . . . . . . . . . . . . . . . . . . . . . . . . .

. . . . . . . . . . . . . . . . . . . . . . . . . . . . . . . . . . . . . . . . . . . . . . . . . . . . . . .

. . . . . . . . . . . . . . . . . . . . . . . . . . . . . . . . . . . . . . . . . . . . . . . . . . . . . . .

. . . . . . . . . . . . . . . . . . . . . . . . . . . . . . . . . . . . . . . . . . . . . . . . . . . . . . .

. . . . . . . . . . . . . . . . . . . . . . . . . . . . . . . . . . . . . . . . . . . . . . . . . . . . . . .

Who Forgot to Lock the Bedroom Door . . . . . . . . . . . . . . . . . . . . . . . . . .

Who Had to Explain What Was Taking Place . . . . . . . . . . . . . . . . . . . . .

Does your child "act up"?

Is your child easily bored?

Is it hard for your child to sit still?

Does your child hit other children?

Is your child always in trouble?

Does your child have a tantrum at bedtime?

Is your child selfish and needy?

Has your child been asked not to return to playgroup?

Do other parents not return your calls?

Has every babysitter you've ever had quit?

Does your child throw tantrums in public?

Does your child torture the pets?

Has your child ever "accidentally" destroyed your own or other
people's property?

Does your child have parents?

Do people leave the room when your child enters it?


If the answer to one or more of these questions is yes, then your
child may be "gifted".

# Does Your Child Have a
# Learning Disability?

Does your child "act up"?

Is your child easily bored?

Is it hard for your child to sit still?

Does your child hit other children?

Is your child always in trouble?

Does your child have a tantrum at bedtime?

Is your child selfish and needy?

Has your child been asked not to return to playgroup?

Do other parents not return your calls?

Has every babysitter you've ever had quit?

Does your child throw tantrums in public?

Does your child torture the pets?

Has your child ever "accidentally" destroyed your own or other
people's property?

Does your child have parents?

Do people leave the room when your child enters it?

If the answer to one or more of these questions is yes, then your
child may have a learning disability.

# Does Your Child Have Attention Deficit Disorder?

Does your child "act up"?

Is your child easily bored?

Is it hard for your child to sit still?

Does your child hit other children?

Is your child always in trouble?

Does your child have a tantrum at bedtime?

Is your child selfish and needy?

Has your child been asked not to return to playgroup?

Do other parents not return your calls?

Has every babysitter you've ever had quit?

Does your child throw tantrums in public?

Does your child torture the pets?

Has your child ever "accidentally" destroyed your own or other people's property?

Does your child have parents?

Do people leave the room when your child enters it?


If the answer to one or more of these questions is yes, then your child may have ADD.

# Do You Have a Pretty Much Average Kid?

Does your child "act up"?

Is your child easily bored?

Is it hard for your child to sit still?

Does your child hit other children?

Is your child always in trouble?

Does your child have a tantrum at bedtime?

Is your child selfish and needy?

Has your child been asked not to return to playgroup?

Do other parents not return your calls?

Has every babysitter you've ever had quit?

Does your child throw tantrums in public?

Does your child torture the pets?

Has your child ever "accidentally" destroyed your own or other

people's property?

Does your child have parents?

Do people leave the room when your child enters it?


If the answer to one or more of these questions is yes, then your

child may be a pretty much average kid.

You can't remember the last time you read a book without pictures in it.

You can't remember the last time you watched a television show that wasn't a cartoon.

You don't think it's unusual to say, "Don't put that in your mouth!" every ten seconds.

If a dummy falls on the floor, it's sterile. If it falls in the toilet, it's dirty.

You've had a serious discussion with your spouse about black and sticky poo versus poo that is green with seeds.

You don't think it's unusual to do ten loads of laundry a week.

You've changed shirts seven times in one day.

You've snuck a dirty nappy into a dustbin in a public place.

You've spelled out a swear word at a business meeting.

You don't think it's unusual to have breast milk in the fridge.

You don't think it's weird to have fourteen kinds of juice in the fridge.

You've started to like eating cereal whose main ingredients are chocolate chips and marshmallow bits.

You can eat an entire meal with one hand.

You don't consider being peed on kinky any more.

You think spitting on a stain and rubbing it is just as good as dry-cleaning.

To Ferber or Not to Ferber

Breast-Feeding, the Graphic Details

Analysing Baby Poo

Bad Grandparent Behaviour

Politically Incorrect Toys

Stroller Storage

Car-Seat Etiquette

Bodily-Fluid Familiarity

Nappy Diagnosis

Diseases Brought Home from Day-Care
   That the Whole Family Will Catch

Scheduling Your Day Around a Nap

The Politics of Playgroup

Overprotective Mums

Underprotective Mums

# What They Used to Talk About

Films

Books

Music

Art

Truth and Beauty

Travel

Fine Wine & Gourmet Food

I figure by the time my husband comes
home at night, if those kids are still alive,
I've done my job.

*—Roseanne*

There are two ways to travel.
First Class or with children.

*—Robert Benchley*

People who say they sleep like a baby
usually don't have one.

*—Leo J. Burke*

Insanity is hereditary –
you get it from your children.

*—Sam Levenson*

Cleaning your house while your kids
are still growing is like shovelling the
walk before it stops snowing.

—*Phyllis Diller*

When I meet a man I ask myself,
"Is this the man I want my children
to spend their weekends with?"

—*Rita Rudner*

All children are essentially criminal.

—*Denis Diderot*

Why can't we have an epidural
after they're born?

—*Anonymous*

JIM MULLEN has written the "Hot Sheet"
column for *Entertainment Weekly* for ten
years. His humour has also appeared in *The New
York Times*, *New York* magazine, and the *Village
Voice*. He is the author of *It Takes a Village
Idiot* and was a contributor to *Paisley Goes with
Nothing* by Hal Rubenstein.

BARRY BLITT is an editorial illustrator and
cartoonist whose work appears in major
magazines in North America and Europe. He
creates cartoons for *Entertainment Weekly*
and is a regular contributor to *The New York
Observer*, *The New Yorker*, *Esquire* and
*The New York Times*.